Celebrating your year

1957

a very special year for

_____

_____

_____

_____

_____

A message from the author:

Welcome to the year 1957.

I trust you will enjoy this fascinating romp down memory lane.

And when you have reached the end of the book, please join me in the battle against AI generated copy-cat books and fake reviews.

Details are at the back of the book.*

Best regards,
Bernard Bradforsand-Tyler.

Contents

Family Life in 1957 America 9
A Decade of Change for the UK 14
Our Love Affair with Cars 17
Tuning in to Television 23
Most Popular TV Shows of 1957 24
The Cold War–Nuclear Arms Race . . . 27
The Cold War–Space Race Begins . . . 29
Prayer Pilgrimage for Freedom 30
Little Rock Nine 31
IRA's Operation Harvest 34
Let a Hundred Flowers Bloom 36
Cinema and Films of 1957 40
Top Grossing Films of 1957 41
A Decade of Cinema Epics 42
Influential Books of 1957 45
West Side Story Hits Broadway 47
Rock 'n' Roll Revolution 49
Billboard Top 30 Songs of 1957 50
Elvis Presley Rocks Our World 52
1950s Fashion Trends 56
Also in Sports 65
In Medicine and Technology 67
Other News from 1957 68
Famous People Born in 1957 72
1957 in Numbers 76
Image Attributions 84

Advertisement

more to see... more to do...   The Vista-Dome California Zephyr
Chicago • Denver • Salt Lake City • Oakland • Sa Francisco

Five Vista-Domes...magnificent mountain scenery...congenial companionship...and plenty to do and see! That's the combination which has made the California Zephyr the most talked-about train in the country!

Choose one of the 120 unreserved Vista-Dome seats, and enjoy unobstructed views of the Colorful Colorado Rockies...the High Sierra...and California's Feather River Canyon—all by daylight. Downstairs, enjoy roomy comfort...delicious meals...delightful refreshments—with your fellow-guests aboard this magnificent train.

Remember...for extra fun at no extra fare...ride the Vista-Dome California Zephyr!

Ask about money-saving family fares!

(Daily through Pullman between New York and San Francisco)
Include Southern California via San Francisco without additional fare
See both Colorado's magnificent Rocky Mountains and California's fabulous Feather River Canyon from Vista-Domes!

Burlington • Rio Grande • Western Pacific

Let's flashback to 1957, a very special year.

Was this the year you were born?

Was this the year you were married?

Whatever the reason, this book is a celebration of your year,

THE YEAR 1957.

Turn the pages to discover a book packed with fun-filled fabulous facts. We look at the people, the places, the politics and the pleasures that made 1957 unique and helped shape the world we know today.

So get your time-travel suit on, and enjoy this trip down memory lane, to rediscover what life was like, back in the year 1957.

It's a washer... It's a dryer... It's two in one!
'57 Philco-Bendix Duomatic

It has happened in your lifetime... a magic hamper!

Just toss your soiled clothes into the Philco-Bendix Duomatic washer-dryer combination. When you come back, they are ready to be worn, ironed or put away. For the Duomatic is a washer and a dryer–it's two in one.

This "miracle" machine actually washes cleaner than any other washer, dries *faster* than any other combination. Think of it! With one setting of the dials, you get clothes that are washed clean, completely dry, sweet-smelling and *sanitized*.

See this beauty at your dealer's. For, if you look ahead, you can't help but choose this wonderful Duomatic for your complete home laundry.

Look ahead... and you'll choose Philco

Family Life in 1957 America

Imagine if time-travel was a reality, and one fine morning you wake up to find yourself flashed back in time, back to the year 1957.

What would life be like for a typical family, in a typical town, somewhere in America?

A camping barbeque–image of a typical middle-class family in 1957.

Our rising middle classes were feeling cashed-up and ready to spend. Consumer demand continued to reach new heights as the post-war boom years delivered us a booming economy, booming birth numbers, booming suburbs, and the booming trappings of the consumerist culture we still aspire to today. An energetic advertising industry, through TV, radio and print, ensured we always knew what our next purchase could and should be.

In the year 1957, the population of the USA increased by 3 million to 177.75 million people.[1]

Increasing demand for single-family homes saw massive suburban developments being built on the outskirts of towns. New home sales were boosted by low interest loans offered to returned soldiers through the G.I. Bill of 1944.

From 1952-1958, 17,300 homes were built in the massive suburban development of Levittown, Pennsylvania.

Our middle-class desires centered around everything new and modern. We just loved to show off our latest purchases and gadgets. Production of goods continued to increase, and businesses were profitable. With only 6.2% of the world's population in 1957,[1] the USA was producing almost half the world's goods.

Joining the television in our families' list of must-haves were: defrost refrigerators, front-loading dryers, fully-automatic washing machines, vacuum cleaners, air-conditioning and heating units, milkshake makers, and a multitude of other kitchen gadgets and home appliances. In addition, we needed a family car, motorcycle, bicycles, hiking equipment, camping and picnic gear, and much, much more.

[1] worldometers.info/world-population/us-population/.

The median family income was $5,000 a year.[1] Unemployment was 5.2% and falling, with GDP growth at 2.1%.[2]

Average costs in 1957 [3]	
New house	$18,904
New car	$2,100
Refrigerator	$250
Vacuum cleaner	$80
A gallon of gasoline	$0.30

But beneath the appearance of domestic bliss, Americans were deeply concerned.

Civil rights activism was on the rise, with a young Martin Luther King Jnr. giving African Americans a voice and national visibility.

The threat of the Soviets was ever present. The Cold War dominated US policies and communist fears gripped the nation throughout the decade and beyond.

By 1957, both super-powers had successfully developed and detonated hydrogen bombs. The Soviets upped the ante—launching a satellite and a dog into space. The nuclear arms race and the space race were underway. We would endure another 34 years of tensions before the Cold War ended with the dissolution of the Soviet Union in 1991.

[1] census.gov/library/publications/1958/demo/p60-029.html.
[2] thebalance.com/unemployment-rate-by-year-3305506.
[3] thepeoplehistory.com and mclib.info/reference/local-history-genealogy/historic-prices/.

Advertisement

On the way to new business–the Voicewriter keeps your office running non-stop

In today's competitive market, the man who lands the business is the man who's on the scene. You have to be free to travel–and at the same time know that back at the office the jobs are getting out.

That's the reason so many executives are turning to the Edison Voicewriter. It lets you turn out correspondence, memos, reports on the go. Just mail the Voicewriter disc to your secretary, and there'll be no backlog waiting when you get back.

You'll discover the Voicewriter's value, back on the home front, too. It helps you get through paperwork in ½ the time. Frees your secretary to do far more valuable work.

Why don't you phone your Edison Business Consultant for a free trial. No obligation. His phone listing is Edison Voicewriter.

- His electronic "secretary" can travel–saves hours of overtime work.
- Your electronic assistant–the Eddison Voicewriter ends duplication of effort...
- frees your secretary to be more of an assistant. And it combines ruggedness with compact design. Buy it! Rent it! The cost? As low as $15.00 a month.

Advertisement

Largest Airliner Ever Built!
Quieter...Faster...More Luxurious
TWA Jetstream

Welcome aboard the great Jetstream *now*! This new Lockheed Starliner offers the quiet of exclusive synchrophased (anti-vibration) propellers, the smoothness of giant, high-altitude wings, the sureness of electronic-eye radar. And the cheerful, colorful Jetstream cabin (above) adds restful luxury...makes your trip seem hours shorter. Non-stop coast to coast, non-stop New York to London/Paris. Reserve space with your TWA travel agent, the nearest TWA ticket office or write 380 Madison Ave., New York 17, N.Y.

Fly the finest   Fly TWA   Trans World Airlines

A Decade of Change for the United Kingdom

Now just imagine you flashed back to a town in 1957 United Kingdom or Western Europe.

Unlike boom-time America, a very different picture would await you.

Many major cities like London bore the brunt of destruction from WWII bombings. The rebuilding process required major loans from the USA and other nations, leaving the UK deep in long-term debt. By 1957, the post-war austerity measures, which had forced the British to tighten their collective belts, were finally loosening up.

Trafalgar Square looking towards Charring Cross railway station, July 1957.

Lack of excess cash reserves made it increasingly difficult for the UK to continue financing and keeping secure its far-flung colonies. As a result, many British colonies would be released during the following ten years, gaining independence as new nations. The United Kingdom was losing its super-power status on the world's stage.

By 1957, job security and record low unemployment meant the middle and working classes were feeling more prosperous and optimistic than they had for a very long time. Living standards were rising and families had money to spend.

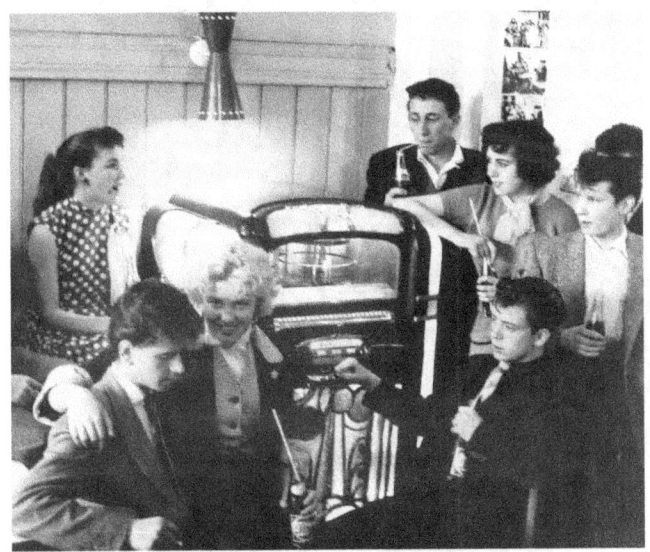

Young adults, and teenagers in particular, had spare cash for leisure and luxuries. Looking for a new voice, the British youth of the mid-'50s turned to American rock 'n' roll music and fashion, giving rise to a distinct youth culture focused on freedom and rebellion.

British teenagers at a party.

Anti Catholic (Anti IRA) loyalist graffiti in Belfast, Northern Ireland, photo taken in 1974.

In Northern Ireland, the IRA (Irish Republican Army) was beginning its Border Campaign–a guerilla styled war against British targets.

Its mission was to overthrow British rule and create a united Ireland. 1957 would be the most active year for the IRA, with 341 incidents recorded. The campaign would continue for another five years without success, enlisting a new generation of fighters to the cause.

Advertisement

Brilliantly New for 1957!

Embodied in the beautiful cars on this page are the most significant automotive advancements we have ever been privileged to present to the motoring public.

Entirely new in design and engineering, and bringing to the world's highways a wholly new standard of quality and excellence–Cadillac for 1957 represents one of the greatest achievements of all time.

The renowned Cadillac stylists have created a brilliant new type of beauty... the master Cadillac coachcrafters have brought a new measure of luxury to the car's interiors... and the world-famous Cadillac engineers have introduced a sensational new concept of automotive performance.

Why not visit your nearest Cadillac dealer at your earliest convenience to see... to inspect... and to drive the new 1957 Cadillac?

It will be a most enlightening experience.

Cadillac Motor Car Division • General Motors Corporation

Our Love Affair with Cars

In 1957, the US was producing more than half of all new vehicles worldwide. Its international domination had peaked in the early '50s, however the car manufacturing industry was now in steady decline.

There were 55.7 million registered cars on US roads, up from 30.7 million ten years earlier.[1] Rising incomes meant the car was no longer considered a luxury reserved only for the wealthy. Our love affair with cars was firmly entrenched.

Customers select from a range of cars on display.

Teenagers at a drive-through in the mid-'50s.

Services related business such as drive-through restaurants and drive-in cinemas were springing up everywhere, especially popular among the younger generation.

[1] www.fhwa.dot.gov/ohim/summary95/mv200.pdf.

Our love affair with cars grew hand-in-hand with the post-war baby boom and housing construction boom. Where would we be without our cars? How else could we get from our suburban homes to our downtown offices?

Car manufacturers competed for our attention with stylish designs, larger engines, and added detailing. The rising middle classes had money to spend, and cars became the ultimate status symbol.

Cars were no longer just a necessity; they had become an expression of our personality. Sturdy, sporty, or luxurious, cars now came in a wide range of styles, colors, and price-points. Decorative chrome and tail fins reached new heights as the decade progressed, with flamboyant wings and stripes for added pizzazz.

To satisfy the '50s consumer desire for style over efficiency and safety, American car manufacturers produced year-on-year bigger, longer and heavier gas-guzzlers. However, by the end of the decade consumers would begin turning against this extravagance and excess.

Advertisement

Step into the wonderful world of AUTODYNAMICS!

Swept·Wing Is Sweeping The Country!

It unleashes a hurricane of power
It breaks through the vibration barrier
It is swept-wing mastery of motion

SWEPT·WING '57 Dodge

It unleashes a hurricane of power   It breaks through the vibration barrier
It is swept-wing mastery of motion

Autodynamics... it holds you snug to the road on curves with race-car torsion bar suspension. This is just one of the sensational benefits of new Torsion-Aire "Realm of Silence" Ride.

Well, it's happened. People who have been "sold" on other makes of cars *for years* are making the swing to the Swept-Wing Dodge.

It took quite a revolution to break them away–and Dodge touched it off with *Autodynamics*.

Here is a world where *everything is new from road to roof* to create a master of motion that teams *sports car lowness* with *limousine luxury*.

It unleashes a hurricane of power from a thundering aircraft-type engine (up to 310 hp.). Tames a tornado of torque with new Push-Button Torque-Flite that packs a silk-smooth 1-2 punch. Breaks through the vibration barrier into a "Realm of Silence" with amazing new Torsion-Aire Ride.

You really should stop in at your Dodge dealer's and find out what's behind the big swing to Swept-Wing. Take a drive and discover the difference. You have never seen, felt, owned anything like it!

Advertisement

Nearly everyone knows by now—
Pontiac's got a Hit!

Seems like everybody's got an eye for this fresh and frisky beauty! And why not? It's a '57 Pontiac, the top crowd pleaser of the year, with over *6 dozen* "firsts" to its credit. There's the all-new "going places" look of Star Flight body design. There's years-ahead riding smoothness with new cradle-soft Level-Line suspension. There are new controls that command instant wheel obedience. Plus a brand-new V-8 engine superior even to last year's world-record Strato-Streak! And when you take all these big-time changes and improvements and polish them to perfection in a rugged *100,000-mile Marathon Run,* you've really got something. You've got, in fact, America's No. 1 Road Car. Come in and try it. You'll be a Pontiac fan for life!

America's number 1 road car!

Four car-producing countries dominated the industry by the start of 1957: England, France, and Germany, with America in the top spot. (Japan had yet to enter this elite group.)

Above: 1957 Dauphine by Renault.
Top: MG Coupé, 1957.
Right: Citroen ID 19, 1957.

America's automotive industry was the largest industry segment in the country, and Detroit was America's car manufacturing powerhouse. The "Big Three" (General Motors, Ford and Chrysler), were all based in the Detroit area. They dominated the industry, having bought out or edged out most of their competitors.

GM Chevrolet assembly line, circa 1955.

By the end of the decade Detroit would become the fifth largest city in the US. A whopping one in six American adults would be employed in the car industry nation-wide.[1]

[1] theweek.com/articles/461968/rise-fall-detroit-timeline.

Advertisement

Presenting Philco HTV
Hyper-Power Television

A picture so much better it demanded a new kid of sound... Wrap-Around Sound

When you turn on a new Philco Hyper-power TV–HTV–you experience a feeling of reality you've never before enjoyed in a TV set! The picture's better, clearer, more powerful than any you've ever seen. And the sound–Philco Wrap-Around Sound–comes to you unbelievably clear and true. Three harmonically balanced speakers, one in front and one on each side (a design exclusive with Philco) bring you every note, every voice inflection. You feel you're there, whether you turn the volume high or prefer it whisper-low.

See and hear new powerful, dependable Philco HTV. There's a complete choice of stunning new cabinets, fine woods skillfully crafted and polished. Your Philco dealer will be glad to demonstrate Philco HTV with Wrap-Around Sound. Philco HTV priced from $179.95.

Look ahead... and you'll choose Philco

Tuning in to Television

By 1957, 78% of US households owned a television set, up from just 9% at the start of the decade.[1] For the rising middle classes, television had become our preferred means of entertainment.

A typical family watching television in the mid-'50s.

The early to mid-'50s is fondly referred to as the first "Golden Age of Television". During this time, live broadcasts from New York City dominated primetime TV. Based on radio and the theatrical traditions of Broadway, these were cheap and quick to produce.

However by 1957, newer formats produced out of Los Angeles were gaining in popularity—sitcoms, soap operas, westerns, crime, medical dramas, and quiz shows, would soon become our primetime staples.

The big Hollywood film studios, having lost much of their viewing public to television, now sought profitable ways to enter the small screen business.

Warner Brothers, 20th Century Fox and MGM invested heavily in made-for-TV shows. By the end of the decade, Hollywood produced programs would dominate primetime TV.

Danny Thomas with Sherry Jackson in *The Danny Thomas Show* (ABC. 1953-'57, CBS. 1957-'64). The family-focused sitcom was filmed by Lucille Ball and Desi Arnaz's Desilu Studios, using the three-camera method invented for *I Love Lucy*. This technique for capturing multiple angles would become the standard for live-audience sitcoms.

[1] americancentury.omeka.wlu.edu/items/show/136.

Most Popular TV Shows of 1957

1. Gunsmoke
2. The Danny Thomas Show
3. Tales of Wells Fargo
4. Have Gun – Will Travel
5. I've Got a Secret
6. The Life and Legend of Wyatt Earp
7. General Electric Theater
8. The Restless Gun
9. December Bride
10. You Bet Your Life
11. The Perry Como Show
12. Alfred Hitchcock Presents
= Cheyenne
14. The Ford Show
15. The Red Skelton Show
16. The Gale Storm Show
17. The Millionaire
18. The Lineup
19. This Is Your Life
= The $64,000 Question

* From the Nielsen Media Research 1957-'58 season of top-rated primetime television series in the USA.

Western drama series *Gunsmoke* ran for 20 seasons, holding the #1 position on Nielsen's ratings for four consecutive years (1957-'60). A total of 635 episodes were created, making *Gunsmoke* the longest-running primetime, live-action television series of the 20th Century.

Five of the top eight TV series of 1957 were western dramas.

Left to Right: Milburn Stone, Ken Curtis, Amanda Blake, and James Arness in *Gunsmoke*.

Long before he was President of the United States, Ronald Reagan was a well know TV personality. As host and part owner of *General Electric Theater* (CBS. 1953-1962), he became known as "The Great Communicator". It is said he developed his public-speaking skills through the many public forums he was invited to speak at.

Richard Boone with Patricia Medina in *Have Gun-Will Travel* (CBS. 1957-1963).

Martin Milner and Vanessa Brown in *Wagon Train* (NBC. 1957-'62, ABC. 1962-'65).

The television networks were quick to turn out new programs to keep us tuning in. Here are just a few of the new programs that aired for the first time in 1957: *Have Gun-Will Travel, Wagon Train, Perry Mason, The Pat Boone Chevy Showroom, The Real McCoys, Leave It to Beaver,* and *The Lucy-Desi Comedy Hour.*

Raymond Burr with Ralph Clanton in *Perry Mason* (CBS. 1957-'66).

Lucille Ball and Desi Arnaz in *The Lucy-Desi Comedy Hour* (CBS. 1957-'60).

Advertisement

New Hit For Busy Holiday Time
...Chun King Frozen Cantonese Dinner

Just like in a fine Cantonese restaurant... an Oriental meal with no work for you

A complete Oriental meal all ready to pop in the oven

It's a holiday in itself–this delightfully different, no-work dinner. Three of those wonderful Chun King American-Oriental foods all dished up for you on a shiny serving tray.

And look at all you get: Two Cantonese egg rolls made from delicate little fresh shrimp, meat, vegetables and fresh eggs wrapped in a crispy-thin pastry. Famous Chun King Chicken Chop Suey with nice big pieces of tender chicken and almonds. Fluffy Oriental white rice. Sound good for *tonight*... and for those holiday busy-times?

This Cantonese Dinner is only one of many Chun King frozen delicacies–everything from chicken chow mein to egg rolls. Chun King is the name that's bringing *new excitement* to frozen food cabinets. Look for it when you shop.

Chun King
The Royalty of American-Oriental Foods

The Cold War–Nuclear Arms Race

Cold War tensions between the two former allies–the USSR and the USA–had been increasing since the end of the war in 1945. Starting in the USA as policies for communist containment, the mutual misunderstanding and distrust escalated from political squabbling to a military Nuclear Arms Race, giving the two superpowers the pretext needed to stockpile and test nuclear bombs on a massive scale.

1957 saw the USA embark on its biggest, most controversial test series carried out on its own soil. *Operation Plumbbob* spanned 4 months, dropping 29 nuclear bombs at the Nevada Proving Grounds. Around 18,000 military personnel were involved, testing their physical and psychological stamina within a nuclear battlefield. In addition, 12,000 pigs were subject to radiation experimentation. Most suffered horrific third degree burns.

By 1957, the US had amassed a stockpile of 5,543 nuclear weapons, against the Soviet's 660. The Soviets upped the ante, confirming the successful development of long range intercontinental ballistic missiles able to reach any corner of the earth.

Both sides continued to increase their nuclear stockpiles. The US peaked in 1967 with a total of 31,225 weapons, against the Soviet's 8,339 weapons.[1] The USSR continued to grow their stockpile until 1988. In 1991, the Nuclear Arms Race ended with the signing of a denuclearization treaty.

[1] tandfonline.com/doi/pdf/10.2968/066004008.

Advertisement

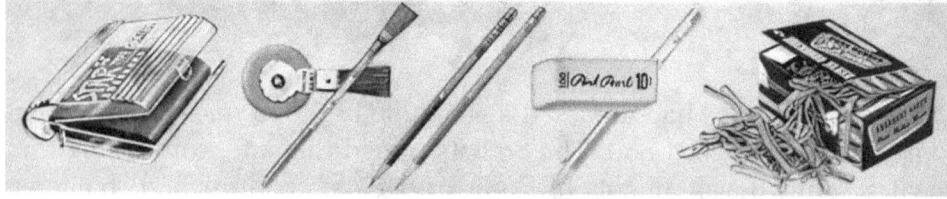

Mongol... the pencil that writes 16,230 words

No wonder 88 per cent of America's writing is done with a woodcased pencil, and no wonder Mongol is America's favorite. Pencil perfect at both ends: a strong, smooth writing lead that keeps a keen point longer... topped by the famous Pink Pearl quality eraser that corrects mistakes in a jiffy. It's America's greatest pencil value, so ask for Mongol by name. Try one today–at better stores everywhere.

Eberhard Faber   10¢ each

puts its quality in writing

The Cold War–Space Race Begins   4th October 1957

It was only about the size of a beach ball and known as Sputnik 1. It was the world's first artificial satellite, launched into earth orbit on 4th October 1957 by the Soviets. The USA-USSR Space Race had begun.

Western newspaper headlines confirming the launch of Sputnik 1.

Following America's announcement of its plan to launch the world's first satellite, the Soviets secretly created the simplest design they could manage to beat the US into space. The 58 cm (23 in.) diameter ball trailed four radio antennas behind it. Two radio transmitters were hidden within, powered by silver-zinc batteries that could last 22 days.

Romanian Commemorative stamp from 1957.

The Soviets followed with Sputnik 2 on 3rd November 1957. Apart from radio and scientific equipment, Sputnik 2 carried a dog named Laika. The part-Samoyed Terrier was fitted with electrodes to monitor her vital signs. There was never any plan to bring Laika home. She died on the third orbit due to overheating.

On 6th December, the US attempted to launch its first satellite–live on TV and radio. Millions watched as the Vanguard rocket carrying the satellite exploded moments after launch. The failed satellite would thereafter be known as *Kaputnik*.

Prayer Pilgrimage for Freedom   17th May 1957

Three years after the US Supreme Court's landmark Brown v. Board ruling, declaring segregation in public schools to be unconstitutional, a crowd of 25,000 gathered at the Lincoln Memorial in Washington D.C. to urge the government to ensure the ruling was upheld. It was the largest organized Civil Rights gathering to date.

Prayer Pilgrimage for Freedom crowd at Lincoln Memorial, 17th May 1957.

Martin Luther King Jnr. Circa 1963.

The three hour event featured prayer, spiritual songs, scripture readings, and speeches. Billed to promote freedom and awareness of the civil rights of African Americans, the event closed with Martin Luther King Jnr. delivering his first address to a national audience. King's impassioned "Give Us the Ballot" speech catapulted the young minister and activist to prominence as the leading voice of the Civil Rights movement.

Little Rock Nine

25th September 1957

Early September 1957, nine African American students enrolled in Little Rock, Arkansas' all-white Central High School. Their attendance would test the Brown v. Board (1954) Supreme Court ruling banning segregation in schools. They would become known as the Little Rock 9.

Under pressure from white parents and pro-segregation groups, Arkansas' schools had continued practicing school segregation, as had most schools in the Southern States and districts elsewhere.

On the first day of classes, Governor Orval Faubus enlisted the Arkansas National Guard to block the teenagers from entering the school. The Governor claimed this was for their own protection. For weeks, the students were harassed, attacked, and prevented from attending classes.

101st Airborne Division soldiers escort the African American students to school.

On 25th September, President Dwight Eisenhower sent 1,200 armed soldiers to maintain peace and ensure the Little Rock Nine could attend a full day of classes.

A rally at Arkansas State Capitol against the admission of black students into Central High School. Protestors waved Confederate flags as the National Guard patrolled. 20th Aug 1959.

The verbal and physical harassment continued, forcing eight of the students to pull out or complete their diplomas through correspondence. Ernest Green was the only Little Rock Nine student to graduate in May 1958.

New York City Mayor Robert Wagner greeting the Little Rock Nine in 1958. From left to right; front row: Minnijean Brown, Elizabeth Eckford, Carlotta Walls, Mayor Robert Wagner, Thelma Mothershed, Gloria Ray; back row: Terrence Roberts, Ernest Green, Melba Pattilo, Jefferson Thomas.

Advertisement

Vintage Airline Posters from 1957.

Advertisement

Can you do this with your camera?

You can if your camera is a Polaroid Land Camera.

For here is the only camera in the world that develops and prints its own pictures in sixty seconds.

And with the remarkable new panchromatic Polaroid Land film, the quality of these pictures is just magnificent. People who see today's Polaroid Land pictures for the first time are absolutely wide-eyed at the sharpness, the sparkle they have.

The Polaroid Land Camera above is one of three new models. It has a coupled rangefinder for automatic focusing, and a self correcting viewfinder that adjusts for near and far pictures.

Polaroid Land Cameras are priced from $72.75. If you prefer, pay only $1.50 a week. Plan on getting one for Christmas.

IRA's Operation Harvest

After decades of sporadic attacks against the British, the Irish Republican Army (IRA) began a five-year border campaign codenamed Operation Harvest. Its aim was to overthrow British rule in Northern Ireland, to create a unified new Ireland.

Beginning in December 1956, the following twelve months of bloody battles made 1957 the most active year in IRA history. A total of 341 acts of guerilla warfare were carried out.

Building attacked during Operation Harvest, 1957.

IRA poster dated Oct 1957.

IRA freedom fighters worked in teams of up to 50 men known as "flying columns". Armed with rifles, sub-machine guns, grenades and bombs, the activists attacked British infrastructure and military bases. However, lacking adequate training and skills, the assaults were often farcical, resulting in injuries and deaths on both sides.

The British swiftly rounded up suspected activists under the Special Powers Act allowing for internment without trial. By year's end, with many hundreds of IRA activists behind bars, including most of their leadership, attacks drastically dwindled.

Operation Harvest was officially called off in 1962. It is remembered by the IRA as a military failure.

Advertisement

Give Keystone Color Movies
All fun... No fuss

The entire family will enjoy Keystone movie-makers... precision-engineered, yet so easily operated. See the complete line at your Keystone dealer's... he offers expert guidance, service, easy budget terms. Movie cameras from $49.95, movie projectors from $74.95, automatic slide-show projectors from $69.95. Make it a Keystone Christmas!

Let a Hundred Flowers Bloom

In February 1957, Chairman Mao Zedong, leader of the Chinese Communist Party, urged the intellectuals of the country to:

> "let a hundred flowers bloom and a hundred schools of thought contend".

This slogan promoted a greater freedom of thought and speech. Individuals were encouraged to give voice to different and competing ideas and opinions, to boost political debate and promote a flourishing of the arts and science through open discussion.

The movement welcomed the submission of letters, proposing ideas, suggestions, or opinions on any topic of concern. For several months Chairman Mao encouraged these submissions, assuring the writers they would not be punished for speaking their truth, even when criticizing the Communist Party or its policies. When Mao began demanding criticisms, the letters flooded in. Students, academics, and even the general public began voicing their frustrations. Topics ranged from difficulties faced in everyday simple activities to condemnation of unjust political policies. Writers even criticized Mao directly.

Propaganda posters for the Hundred Flowers movement, 1957.

Perhaps Chairman Mao assumed he was too perfect to receive criticism. Or perhaps the Hundred Flowers movement was a trap designed to catch liberals and anti-communists.

By June '57, Mao pivoted sharply against the writers. He asserted that not all criticisms were to be tolerated. Those who had openly criticized him and the Communist Party, were labelled as Rightists, and soon would feel his wrath.

A propaganda poster for the Hundred Flowers movement, 1957, showing Chairman Mao surrounded by adoring Chinese citizens.

Chairman Mao Zedong on an airplane, circa 1957.

An Anti-Rightists Campaign began in July '57. Hundreds of thousands of rightists were rounded up. At best they lost their jobs. At worst they were executed, or sent to reform through labor camps, where they were forced to perform hard labor for years or decades.

The total removal of intellectuals and the fear of speaking out led to the disastrous social experiment that was China's Great Leap Forward (1958-1960). Tens of millions starved to death during the flawed campaign, however no-one dared challenge Mao's irrational logic.

The arrest of a suspected Rightist in the wake of the Hundred Flowers campaign, 1957.

Advertisement

"That cactus makes me thirsty... let's have more Postum!"

Enjoy Postum, the hot drink with a different flavor...

"That cactus makes me thirsty... let's have more Postum!"

It's fun, looking at the color slides of your vacation, and Postum is fun too. Postum is a pleasant holiday from everyday hot drinks.

You'll enjoy the *difference* of Postum's grain-rich, slow-roasted flavor. And you'll find Postum helps you top an evening at home–or away–with a good night's sleep. Postum is 100% caffein-free, equally safe for you *and* your children.

For less than a penny a cup, enjoy this pleasantly *different* hot drink this very evening.

Enjoy Postum, the hot drink with a different flavour...

Advertisement

...you can find the answers to your questions in

Today's Encyclopedia **AMERICANA**

When Lincoln didn't know the answer... he turned to his Encyclopedia Americana
...*you* can find the answers to your questions in *Today's Encyclopedia Americana*

A century ago, when Abraham Lincoln was a rather obscure Illinois lawyer-politician still at the threshold of destiny, his scanty library of cherished books included the 1851 edition of The Encyclopedia Americana.

This typifies the respect for learning which is at the heart of our democratic tradition. Since 1820 *The Americana* has provided information and inspiration for leaders of our nation—in government, industry, science, the arts and professions.

Today, this handsome and compact 30-volume library places the accumulated knowledge of man at *your* fingertips—modern knowledge because the latest, most modern edition is the culmination of Americana's great program of revision. Leading scholars from all over the free world have collaborated to bring you authentic information on almost every conceivable subject. More than 60,000 articles and 11,000 illustrations, and everything is easy to find and absorbing to read.

Of course, we can't all be Lincolns, but you and your family deserve the best... the fullest opportunity to a happier, richer life!

30 *great volumes*   *Priced from* $299.50—in backram binding... to $600.00—for the magnificently designed, rich, deep maroon, full leather binding—a set of striking beauty.

Cinema and Films of 1957

Left to Right: Rock Hudson, John Wayne and Kim Novak studio portraits from the '50s.

From its peak in the mid-1940s, cinema attendance faced a steady decline as the television set took pride of place in nearly every household. By 1957, cinemas were struggling to stay profitable, and many were forced to close. The motion picture industry needed to find creative ways to win over new audiences.

The rise of big budget epic films, such as *The Ten Commandments* (1956), *War and Peace* (1956) and *The Bridge on the River Kwai* (1957), took advantage of the new, bigger screen formats offered by VistaVision, Cinerama and Cinemascope, to lure back viewers.

Highest Paid Stars of 1957

1. Rock Hudson
2. John Wayne
3. Pat Boone
4. Elvis Presley
5. Frank Sinatra
6. Kim Novak
7. Gary Cooper
8. William Holden
9. James Stewart
10. Jerry Lewis

Catherine Deneuve publicity photo.

1957 film debuts

Alan Arkin — Calypso Heat Wave
Catherine Deneuve — The Twilight Girls
Andy Griffith — A Face in the Crowd
Lee Remick — A Face in the Crowd
Liv Ullmann — Fjols til fjells

* From en.wikipedia.org/wiki/1957_in_film.

Top Grossing Films of 1957

1	The Bridge on the River Kwai	Columbia Pictures	$15,000,000
2	Peyton Place	20th Century Fox	$11,000,000
3	Sayonara	Warner Bros.	$10,500,000
4	Search for Paradise	CRC	$6,500,000
5	Old Yeller	Walt Disney/Beuna Vista	$5,900,000
6	Raintree County	MGM	$5,830,000
7	Island in the Sun	20th Century Fox	$5,000,000
=	A Farewell to Arms	20th Century Fox	$5,000,000
8	Pal Joey	Columbia Pictures	$4,700,000
9	Gunfight at the O.K. Corral	Paramount Pictures	$4,300,000
10	Don't Go Near the Water	MGM	$4,265,000

* From en.wikipedia.org/wiki/1957_in_film by box office gross in the USA.

Winning 4 of its 10 Academy Award nominations, *Sayonara* bravely tackled race relations at a time when inter-race marriage was still illegal in the US.

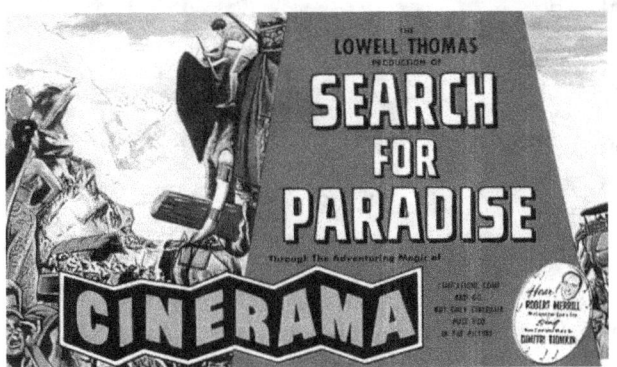

Island in the Sun similarly engaged in themes of interracial romance, while focusing on the social and political inequalities between the white, black and native races on the fictional island of Santa Marta.

A Decade of Cinema Epics

The 1950s saw cinema studios take big risks with extravagant and spectacular epic films. Exotic locations, expensive sets, multiple A-list actors and casts of thousands ensured big ticket sales at the box office. The films of 1957 did not disappoint, with several splendid epics among the highest grossing films of the year.

Alec Guinness as Lieutenant Colonel Nicholson in David Lean's *The Bridge on the River Kwai* (Columbia Pictures, 1957).

The epic war film *The Bridge on the River Kwai* is widely considered to be one of the greatest films of all time.

Based on the 1952 novel by Pierre Boulle, and directed by David Lean, the plot follows British POWs in Japanese camps, forced to construct the Burma Railway during WWII.

The film was a success with the critics and at the box office, winning seven Academy Awards from eight nominations. In addition, the film won four BAFTA Awards from the British Academy.

In 1997, the US Library of Congress selected the film for preservation in the National Film Registry, due to its cultural, aesthetic, and historical significance.

Rock Hudson, Hollywood's number 1 leading man of the '50s, starred in two historical epics released in 1957.

Set during WWI, *A Farewell to Arms* follows the tragic love story of American Officer Frederick Henry (Rock Hudson) and British nurse Catherine Barkley (Jennifer Jones). Based on Ernest Hemingway's 1929 novel of the same name, the film was shot on location in the Italian Alps and Rome using wide-screen DeLuxe Color CinemaScope film. Apart from the beauty of the Alps, the big budget epic was generally panned by critics and has largely been forgotten over time.

Hudson's second war epic for 1957 was the biopic *Battle Hymn*, based on the real life of ex-fighter pilot turned minister Dean Hess (Rock Hudson).

Set during the Korean War, Hess had volunteered to train pilots in South Korea. He soon found himself protecting hundreds of orphaned children, eventually establishing an orphanage for them.

The movie was well received, but not the box office sensation Hudson had hoped for. Hess donated all the profits from his memoir and the movie to the orphanage he founded.

Advertisement

Now! Fly SABENA to the heart of Paris
...the world's first New York-to-Europe service of its kind...with an exclusive helicopter flight from Brussels...at no extra fare

SABENA BELGIAN *World* AIRLINES
SETS THE PACE IN MODERN AIR TRAVEL

Serving 96 key cities in Europe, Africa and the Middle East.

Deluxe Sabena service. Only Sabena takes you and your luggage in a 12-passenger helicopter to the center of Paris, almost on the doorstep of your hotel. Mlle. Sabena, of the world-famous Lady Sabena Club, meets your plane... helps speed luggage through customs... solves any number of your personal problems.

Now! Fly Sabena to the heart of Paris... the world's first New York-to-Europe service of its kind... with an exclusive helicopter flight from Brussels... at no extra fare

This spring Sabena adds a unique experience to your European trip by landing you in the middle of Paris, minutes from the Eiffel Tower. Sabena's new service costs no more than other New York-to-Paris flights, whether you travel First Class or Tourist.

You start your trip to Europe in the world's newest, fastest American-built airliner—the luxurious DC-7C—non-stop from New York to Brussels. Waiting for you there is a giant Sikorsky S-58 helicopter to fly you direct to downtown Paris. On the way, you see the rolling countryside and quaint villages of Belgium and France, then a bird's-eye view of the Arch of Triumph, Notre Dame and all of Paris. You can be one of the first Americans to have this adventure.

For reservations and a colorful free folder about this new service, see your Travel Agent, he's an expert... Make your reservations now, to be sure you are one of the first to enjoy this new service which starts March 1, 1957.

Belgian World Airlines sets the pace in modern air travel.
Serving 96 key cities in Europe, Africa and the Middle East.

Influential Books of 1957

Celebrated children's author Dr. Seuss (Theodor Seuss Geisel), released two of his most loved titles in 1957; *The Cat in the Hat* and *How The Grinch Stole Christmas*. Both books continue to be best sellers today.

1957 was a remarkable year for literature, with some of the century's most influential titles released. Here is a selection of some of '57s best titles, many of which have been retold in film, and continue to be loved by readers and studied by academics as literary masterpieces.

Alistair MacLean's thrilling epic adventure war novel *The Guns of Navarone* was hugely successful upon release. The film, released four years later, starring Gregory Peck, David Niven and Anthony Quinn, was equally well received.

Jack Kerouac's *On the Road* was a defining text of the American Beat Generation.

Boris Pasternak's *Dr. Zhivago*, a 500 page tragic tale of love amidst the backdrop of war in Russia, was immediately banned in the USSR. The book won the Nobel Prize for Literature, causing a political uproar. Pasternak was threatened with arrest and prevented from leaving the country to collect his Nobel Prize.

In 1965, a film adaptation was released starring Omar Sharif.

Advertisement

A new Royal Portable can raise her marks up to 38%

It happens every day! Many so called "slow students" learn to type and then show up on the honor roll.

Incredible? Not at all. Typing makes homework fun, actually encourages study, helps organize lessons, helps finish assignments faster.

Start them right with Royal! Twin-Pak, the quick-change, no-smudge ribbon... Magic Margin... extra light touch... that famous Royal ruggedness! These are just a few of the exclusives that make the 1957 Royal Portable the greatest portable that ever went to school–the all-time favorite of students.

Pay just Pennies a day! You can buy a Royal Portable in any one of the 6 wonderful colors for only a few pennies a day, with up to two full years to pay. There's nothing to keep you from giving your student a new Royal Portable–and a Royal send-off toward better grades–*right now*.

Convenience plus! Only the new Royal Portable gives you Twin-Pak ribbon. Changes instantly–no messy fingers.

Royal   *world's most wanted portable typewriter*

West Side Story Hits Broadway

26th September 1957

West Side Story, the hugely successful 1957 Broadway musical by Leonard Bernstein and Stephen Sondheim, opened at the Winter Garden Theatre on 26th September, playing for 732 performances before going on tour.

Stabbing scene, original Broadway cast of *West Side Story*, 1957.

Loosely based on the forbidden love story of Shakespeare's *Romeo and Juliet*, *West Side Story* tackled the darker themes of gang violence and racial tensions. Set in Manhattan's Upper West Side, the gritty sets and frequent use of common street slang was groundbreaking in the musical genre. The musical was well received by the critics and the young, but not by Broadway's older, more conservative theater goers.

Larry Kent as Tony, in the original Broadway cast of *West Side Story*, 1957.

"I Feel Pretty" sung by Carol Lawrence as Maria, with cast members.

A 1961 film version, starring Natalie Wood, won 10 Academy Awards including Best Picture. A second film adaptation, directed by Steven Spielberg, was released in 2021.

Advertisement

IT SAYS YOU'RE GOING PLACES...

A—The Hardy. Pink with charcoal; sandalwood with terra cotta; 2-tone green. (8BX5) $29.95. B—The Trooper. "Wavefinder." 2-tone grey; white with turquoise; 2-tone blue. (8BX6) $34.95. C—The Gentry. Precision tuner. "Wavefinder." Aqua; pink; grey. (6BX1) $39.95. D—The New "Globe Trotter." Extra power. "Wavefinder." Merino grey or aqua. (7BX9) $45.95.

Sleek, rugged new RCA Victor portables in the non-breakable "Impac" case

NON-BREAKABLE "IMPAC" CASE can really take it! Won't split, crack or chip even when dropped (shown). Guaranteed for 5 years.

"WAVEFINDER" ANTENNA. Now the speaker can always face you. Instead of turning the set for best reception, just flip the "Wavefinder."

You can feel the excitement.

You're carrying a new RCA Victor portable—and somehow even a stroll seems like you're going places. Other people sense it, too—the dash, the youthful look and *feel!*

There's a bold sweep to these beautiful new portables. There's a youthful nonchalance about the non-breakable "IMPAC" case, that simply shrugs off punishment. In fact, the case is *guaranteed for a full five years* of normal use!

You enjoy New Sensations in Sound, too. Each of those colorful portables brings you famous "Golden Throat" tone for rich console-like sound. For economical operation, each plays on AC or DC current as well as on batteries. Most models have the "Wavefinder" antenna that gives you best reception at the touch of a finger.

To see what we mean, start going places now—and make the first step your RCA Victor dealer's.

RCA VICTOR
CAMDEN 2, NEW JERSEY

It says you're going places...
Sleek, rugged new RCA Victor portables in the non-breakable "Impac" case
You can feel the excitement.
  You're carrying a new RCA Victor portable–and somehow even a stroll seems like you're going places. Other people sense it, too–the dash, the youthful look and *feel!*
  There's a bold sweep to these beautiful new portables. There's a youthful nonchalance about the non-breakable "Impac" case that simply shrugs off punishments. In fact, the case is *guaranteed for a full five years* of normal use!
  You enjoy New Sensations in Sound, too. Each of these colorful portables brings you famous "Golden Throat" tone for rich console-like sound. For economical operation, each plays on AC or DC current as well as on batteries. Most models have the "Wavefinder" antenna that gives you best reception at the touch of a finger...
  Non-Breakable "Impac" Case can really take it!
Won't split, crack or chip even when dropped... Guaranteed for 5 years.
  "Wavefinder" Antenna. Now the speaker can always face you.
Instead of turning the set for best reception, just flip the "Wavefinder."

Rock 'n' Roll Revolution

Rock 'n' roll exploded onto our soundwaves in the mid-fifties, and took the world by storm. It burst from the ghettos, from small town local record studios, while the big city record labels were napping. The energy, the rhythm, the emotion—we had never heard anything quite like it before. Parents were alarmed and appalled in equal measure.

Rock 'n' roll greats: Chuck Berry, Fats Domino, and Jerry Lee Lewis.

Rock 'n' roll was the first music ever created specifically for teenagers. The first of the Baby Boomers had found their sound. It was neither black nor white. It gave expression to youth of any race and social status. It was a mash of rhythm & blues, country & western, gospel, hill-billy, blues, and jazz, with a heavy rock beat.

Sun Records in Memphis, Tennessee, was home to many rock 'n' roll greats, including Elvis Presley, Jerry Lee Lewis, Carl Perkins, Jonny Cash, Roy Orbison, and Howlin' Wolf. Founder Sam Phillips is widely recognized as an influential pioneer in the rock 'n' roll genre.

5th Aug 1957 – *American Bandstand* with host Dick Clark broadcast nationally, bringing the top charting singles into our homes. The weekly TV show would be successfully syndicated for the next 32 years.

Billboard Top 30 Songs of 1957

	Artist	Song Title
1	Elvis Presley	All Shook Up
2	Pat Boone	Love Letters in the Sand
3	The Diamonds	Little Darlin'
4	Tab Hunter	Young Love
5	Jimmy Dorsey	So Rare
6	Pat Boone	Don't Forbid Me
7	Guy Mitchell	Singing the Blues
8	Sonny James	Young Love
9	Elvis Presley	Too Much
10	Perry Como	Round and Round

Elvis Presley.

Pat Boone, 1960.

Perry Como, 1956.

Debbie Reynolds, 1964.

	Artist	Song Title
11	The Everly Brothers	Bye Bye Love
12	Debbie Reynolds	Tammy
13	Buddy Knox	Party Doll
14	Elvis Presley	Teddy Bear
15	Harry Belafonte	Day-O (The Banana Boat Song)
16	Elvis Presley	Jailhouse Rock
17	Marty Robbins	A White Sport Coat (and a Pink Carnation)
18	The Del-Vikings	Come Go with Me
19	The Everly Brothers	Wake Up Little Susie
20	Sam Cooke	You Send Me

The Everly Brothers, 1958.

Harry Belafonte, 1954.

	Artist	Song Title
21	The Coasters	Searchin'
22	Chuck Berry	School Days
23	Ferlin Husky	Gone
24	Paul Anka	Diana
25	Ricky Nelson	A Teenager's Romance
26	The Tarriers	The Banana Boat Song
27	Jimmie Rodgers	Honeycomb
28	Jerry Lee Lewis	Whole Lotta Shakin' Goin On
29	Gale Storm	Dark Moon
30	The Crickets	That'll Be the Day

* From the *Billboard* top 30 singles of 1957.

Elvis Presley Rocks Our World

Elvis Presley burst onto our collective consciousness in January 1956 ushering in the age of Rock 'n' roll. By the end of the year, he had sold 10 million singles, accounting for half of all sales at RCA Victor, the largest record label in the US at that time. His performances were wild events, with hoards of screaming young fans, often requiring the National Guard standing by to control the crowds.

Presley began 1957 with his third and final performance on *The Ed Sullivan Show* (CBS). Cameramen were instructed to shoot the singer from the waist up, avoiding his sexually provocative trademark grinding gyrations, which Sullivan had deemed "unfit for family viewing", and earned Presley the moniker "Elvis the Pelvis".

Rather than continue with the TV bookings and grueling live shows (143 live concerts in 1956), Presley pivoted in 1957 to focus on an acting career.

Elvis Presley in St. Louis, March 1957, with some local fans.

Presley signed a seven-year contract with Paramount Pictures, releasing his first film, *Love Me Tender*, at the end of 1956. He would star in two more movies during 1957–*Loving You* and *Jailhouse Rock*. The movies established the formula for future Presley movies—light romantic comedies with silly plot lines, sprinkled with musical numbers. A pre-released soundtrack ensured strong box office sales.

Presley would star in 31 feature films during his acting career. Although none were critically acclaimed, they were always a hit with his fans and financially successful for the film studio.

In March '57, Presley purchased *Graceland*, an 18-room mansion in Memphis, Tennessee. He paid $102,500, using royalties from his straight run of #1 singles and albums. The home is now a public museum and has been declared a National Historic Landmark. 650,000 visitors a year make *Graceland* the most visited private home in the US.

Graceland, front entrance, 2018.

Jailhouse Rock recording sessions, May 1957.

By the end of 1957, four of the top twenty Billboard songs of the year belonged to Elvis Presley. He was more idolized by his fans than ever, and his popularity would see him through two years of absence from the spotlight. On 20th December, Presley received his draft notice.

Presley returned from military duty in 1960 and continued right where he had left off, releasing a string of #1 hit songs and more fun and frivolous films.

Presley died in 1977 following years of prescription drug abuse.

Presley broke the boundaries during racially segregated '50s America. His sound appealed to black and white listeners, crossing several genres. He was posthumously inducted into 5 Music Halls of Fame, including those for Country Music, Gospel Music, and Rockabilly.

Presley continues to rank as one of the highest earning deceased celebrities, in large part due to merchandise sales, tours of *Graceland*, and re-releases of his songs.

Advertisement

Keep those precious "growing up" words on your Webcor High Fidelity Tape Recorder

Now you can keep a priceless sound album as your child grows up—recorded on a Webcor High Fidelity Tape Recorder.

And that's only the beginning. A Webcor Tape Recorder adds a new kind of fun to parties. It's marvelous for practicing music lessons or speeches—because you can really hear yourself as others hear you! And what a thrill to record your favorite radio and TV programs—and play them back whenever you want a repeat performance.

So very important, too—your Webcor gives you the very finest high fidelity reproduction of the many popular and classical pre-recorded tapes now available, as well as the tapes you record yourself.

Ask your dealer to demonstrate Webcor's many advantages—including the famous "no reel-turnover" feature.

A. Royal Tape Recorder. High fidelity; wide-range speaker; two recording heads... $199.95.
B. Royal Coronet Tape Recorder-Radio... three speakers... Supersensitive AM radio tuner... $289.95.
C. Viscount Tape Recorder. High fidelity; full-range PM speaker; 5-tube amplifier; professional type editing button. 5 watts power output, and many other features... Only $149.95.

All music sounds better on a Webcor

Advertisement

Dresses from the *Sears Roebuck Home Order Catalog*, Summer 1957.

1950s Fashion Trends

With the penny-pinching misery and bleakness of the war years behind us, the 1950s were a time to show off. And nowhere was this more apparent than through our fashion choices. The pinched waist look of the late '40s carried throughout the '50s. Our clothes allowed us to express beauty, excellence, luxury and extravagance.

Fashion of the '50s was highlighted by a clear gender divide. While women's fashion focussed on femininity and tailored formality, men's fashion embraced the casual and cool of working class daywear.

By the mid-'50s, dresses and skirts reached voluminous proportions, with pleats and folds flaunting an abundance of fabric.

Christian Dior's "New Look" from 1947.

Day wear and evening wear for women on both sides of the Atlantic continued to take its direction from the haute couture salons of Paris. Christian Dior's "New Look", unveiled in 1947, set the standard for the entire decade of the 1950s.

Gone were the boxy tailored jackets with padded shoulders and short skirts. Dior had brought back femininity, with clinched waists, fuller busts and hips, and longer, wider skirts. The emphasis was on abundance.

Christian Dior's "New Look" in the mid-'50s.

To achieve this impossible hourglass figure, corsets and girdles were sold in record numbers. Metal underwire bras made a comeback, and a new form of bra known as the "cathedral bra" or "bullet bra" became popular.

Fabulous Figuring by Formfit, 1956.

Women embraced the femininity of 1950s fashion from head to toe. Hats, scarves, belts, gloves, shoes, stockings, handbags and jewelry were all given due consideration.

Out on the street, no outfit was complete without a full complement of matching accessories.

A little of the Lady vanishes in Merry Widow by Warner's

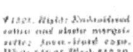

If you're the (daring) darling of your group, you know that if it isn't by Warner's, it just isn't a Merry Widow®. After all, Merry Widow was invented by Warner's. Each year they bring out exciting new versions of this charmer—to mold you under the latest looks. Here, for instance, two of the season's most scintillating—in the 1912 mood, and as essential to gala evenings as your most captivating smile.

WARNER'S
BRAS · GIRDLES · CORSELETTES

A little of the Lady vanishes in Merry Widow by Warner's

If you're the (daring) darling of your group, you know that if it isn't by Warner's, it just isn't a Merry Widow. After all, Merry Widow was invented by Warner's. Each year they bring out exciting new versions of this charmer–to mold you under the latest looks. Here, for instance, two of the season's most scintillating–in the 1912 mood, and as essential to gala evenings as your most captivating smile.

Warners
Bras • Girdles • Corselettes

Despite criticisms against the extravagance of the New Look, and arguments that heavy corsets and paddings undermined the freedoms women had won during the war years, the New Look was embraced on both sides of the Atlantic.

Dresses from the *Sears and Roebucks Spring Catalog*, 1957.

Clothing manufacturers produced stylish, ready-to-wear clothes for the masses. Inexpensive versions of Dior's New Look in florals and pretty pastels filled our closets and graced our suburban homes and streets. No longer just for the wealthy, the growing middle classes could now afford to be fashionable. Magazines and mail-order catalogs were sure to keep us informed of the latest in fashion and accessories.

Advertisement

Cashmere Punched Pig: Fashion's Newest Pet

This is spring's smartest look—for busy suburban living or active dashing about town. The richly grained texture of Punched Pig... perfect punctuation for your separates, your casual suits and toppers. And you'll love them for their soft and wonderful *feel*... for the gentle *fit* you've learned to expect of Cobbies. Styles illustrated: above, Rustic; bottom left, Tally-Ho; right, Roundtowner Tie.

Available at fine stores everywhere... write, we'll tell you where.
Smart young Cobbies 8.95 to 11.95

Cobbies
A Red Cross Shoe

Dior also created a slimmed down alternative look, widely copied by other designers in ready-to-wear and pattern books. This figure-hugging, groomed and tailored look continued to place emphasis on the hourglass figure, and was suitable for day or evening dress, or as an elegant straight skirt and short jacket.

Known as the "sheath dress" or "wiggle dress", this sexier silhouette was preferred by movie stars such as Jane Russell and Marilyn Monroe.

Model wears Dior inspired outfit by Forstmann.

Dress patterns by Advance.

Marilyn Monroe in 1957.

Not much changed in the world of men's fashion during the 1950s. Business attire shifted just a little. Suits were slimmer, and ties were narrower. Skinny belts were worn over pleated pants. Hats, though still worn, were on the way out.

Marlon Brando.

Frank Sinatra.

Elvis Presley.

For the younger generation, the fashion icons of the day set the trends. Elvis Presley in the mid-'50s presented a clean-cut casual elegance. The perfectly swept hair and open Cuban-collar bowling shirt became his signature.

James Dean and Marlon Brando made the white T-shirt and blue jeans the must-have items in casual attire. Worn alone, or under an unbuttoned shirt or jacket, the look made working class style a middle-class fashion statement.

Advertisement

The Acapulco High Divers by Jantzen

Here are three great new Jantzen swimming and diving trunks, inspired–and tested–by the famous cliff divers of Acapulco. They fit perfectly, stay comfortable and look good all day, no matter how high the dive or how rough the surf. Choose yours from the trim red trunks (left) of strong, elasticized fabric, 5.95... the handsome multi-stripe (center) with elasticized waist for snug fit, 5.95... or the neat white trunks (right) with elastic waistband, 4.95. In all sizes, your favorite colors–at the better stores.

Jantzen
sportswear for sportsmen

Also in Sports

11th March– Thousands rioted at a soccer match in Bari, Italy, when a clash broke out between fans of teams Bari and Tananto.

28th May– National League baseball approved the relocation of the New York Giants and Brooklyn Dodgers to the US west coast. They would become the San Francisco Giants and Los Angeles Dodgers.

6th July– American tennis champion Althea Gibson became the first black athlete to win Wimbledon, beating Darlene Hard 6-3, 6-2. Two months later, at the US Open, Gibson became the first black athlete to win a major US tennis tournament.

Darlene Hard congratulating Althea Gibson upon her winning the 1957 Wimbledon Women's Singles Championship. Hard and Gibson were doubles partners and 1957 Wimbledon Women's Doubles Champions.

6th -10th June– Louise Suggs won the LPGA Championship, becoming the first golfer to obtain the Career Grand Slam (after winning the U.S. Women's Open, Western Open and Titleholders Championship).

Juan Manuel Fangio after his 1955 F1 win in Netherlands.

20th July– French Jacques Anquetil won the 4,665 km Tour de France. He would go on to win the race five times.

4th August– Argentine Maserati driver Juan Manuel Fangio won the German Grand Prix at Nürburgring, his 5th Formula 1 Championship.

Advertisement

"Super-7" Clippers are the world's fastest and quietest over-ocean airliners.

Don't envy them... *Go!*

Oh, these lucky people–off on a big day by "Super-7" Clipper! Next stop: London? Paris? Hawaii?

For people who just can't wait to start their vacations, nothing equals Pan American's giant "Super-7" Clippers–Douglas-built DC-7Cs–fastest over-ocean airliners in the world.

And *speed* is only part of the beauty of Pan Am's "Super-7s." Whisper across the aisle; you can be heard. It is remarkably quiet, thanks to triple-thick windows and extra soundproofing... coupled with the fact that the engines are mounted five feet farther away from the cabin. With radar to probe the weather 150 miles out front, your "Super-7" flies the smoothest, fairest weather routes.

No other airline in the world comes close in size to Pan Am's mighty fleet of DC-7Cs. Out of a grand total of 77 weekly flights to Europe, 41 are "Super-7s"; out of 41 to Hawaii, 23 are "Super-7s." They're yours on tourist-fare *Rainbow* and first-class *President* service. Call your Travel Agent or Pan Am.

World's most experienced airline   Pan American

In Medicine and Technology

February 1957– A H2N2 influenza outbreak spread from Asia to other continents. Known as the Asian Flu Pandemic, it was the second major influenza pandemic of the century, claiming over 150,000 lives.

April 1957– Fortran, an early computer language, was commercially released by IBM. The user-friendly software was developed to streamline and simplify the process of computer programming.

27th June– The Medical Research Council of UK published a special report confirming a direct link between smoking and lung cancer. The study analyzed lung cancer rates over a 25-year period.

1st July– The International Geophysical Year (IGY) commenced, involving 67 countries, to promote research and advances in rocketry, radar, and computing over an 18-month period. The IGY contributed directly to the development of the Antarctic Treaty, the discovery of Van Allen radiation belts, and a fuller understanding of plate-tectonic theory.

31st October– Toyota established a US company to sell its cars on the US market. Cars began shipping from Japan the following year.

18th December– The Shippingport Atomic Power Station in Pennsylvania, USA, was connected to the power grid, making it the world's first full scale nuclear power plant built solely to generate electricity.

December 1957– Dr. Ian Donald of University of Glasgow, Scotland, pioneered the use of diagnostic ultrasound scanning with the aim to detect abnormalities during pregnancy. Modern ultrasound machines are still in use today.

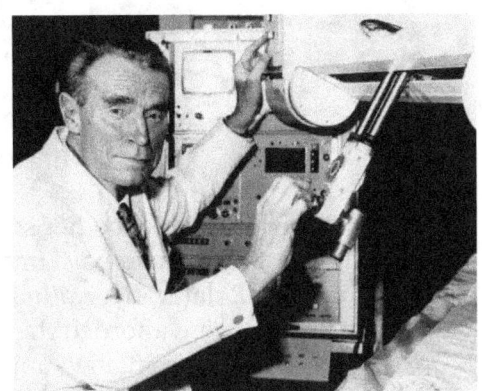

Other News from 1957

10th January– Harold Macmillan was appointed Prime Minister of the United Kingdom following the resignation of Anthony Eden.

Inventor Walter Frederick Morrison promoting his Pluto Platter.

23rd January– Toy company Wham-O released the Pluto Platter. The popular device would later become known as the Frisbee.

4th March– The Standard & Poor 500 (S&P 500) stock market index was introduced, tracking the performance of 500 large companies listed on US stock exchanges. It replaced the more limited S&P 90.

25th March– The Treaty of Rome was signed by West Germany, France, Belgium, Italy, Luxembourg, and the Netherlands establishing the European Economic Community, the precursor to the European Union.

6th April– Greek shipping tycoon Aristotle Onassis bought the TAE Greek National Airlines and renamed the company Olympic Airlines.

14th July– Rawya Ateya took her seat at the National Assembly of Egypt, becoming the first female parliamentarian in the Arab world. She was joined one week later by Amina Shukri. It was the first year that Egyptian women were afforded the right to vote and be eligible for office. 70% of Egyptian men remained opposed to women in Parliament.

17th September– Actress Sophia Loren married her agent Carlo Ponti. As the Catholic Church did not recognize Ponti's previous divorce, he was charged with bigamy, and the pair were forced to annul their marriage. They remarried in 1975 after becoming French Citizens.

6th November– US President Dwight D. Eisenhower was re-elected for a second term, defeating Democrat candidate Adlai Stevenson.

22nd October– François "Papa Doc" Duvalier was elected President of Haiti. The autocratic and despotic ruler declared himself President for Life. He ruled till his death in 1971.

4th December– A commuter steam train collided with a stationary electric train in heavy fog near Lewisham, England, killing 92 and injuring 173. The crash dislodged carriages from the track, slamming into an overhead bridge pier, causing the bridge to collapse onto the stationary train.

Advertisement

"My daddy goes a hundred thousand million miles away sometimes, but he always calls us up and makes us feel good"

Bell Telephone System
Call by Number, It's Twice as Fast.

Long Distance Rates are Low

Station-to-Station Rates

For example:	First 3 minutes	Each Added Minute
Baltimore to New York	55¢	15¢
Milwaukee to Des Moines	75¢	20¢
Indianapolis to Memphis	85¢	25¢
Los Angeles to Salt Lake City	1.05¢	30¢
Chicago to Denver	1.30¢	35¢

These rates apply every night after 6 and all day Sunday. Add the 10% federal excise tax.

Advertisement

TIME-SAVING TWOSOME

Whatever your figuring need, there's a Burroughs Adding Machine with the right features, the right capacity and the right price for you. For Burroughs has the most complete line of adding machines in the business—a line featuring the compact Ten-Key and the full-keyboard Director. For a demonstration call our local branch or dealer today. Burroughs Division, Burroughs Corporation, Detroit 32, Mich.

BURROUGHS ADDING MACHINES

Time-Saving Twosome

Whatever your figuring need, there's a Burroughs Adding Machine with the right features, the right capacity and the right price for you. For Burroughs has the most complete line of adding machines in the business—a line featuring the compact Ten-Key and the full-keyboard Director. For a demonstration call our local branch or dealer today.

See the new Thriftline too!
Smart, low-cost adding machines by Burroughs.
Hand-operated. Finished in attractive Amber Gray.

Famous People Born in 1957

6th Jan– Nancy Lopez, American golfer (3 majors, 48 LPGA wins).

12th Jan– John Lasseter, American animation director (Pixar).

17th Jan– Steve Harvey, American actor, comedian, TV & radio personality.

28th Jan– Frank Skinner, English comedian.

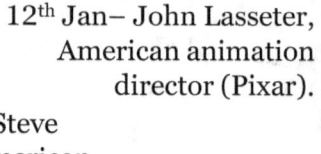

10th Mar– Osama bin Laden, Islamic militant & founder of al-Qaeda, Saudi Arabia (d. 2011).

20th Mar– Spike Lee [Shelton Jackson Lee], American film director.

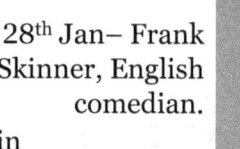

1st Apr– David Gower, English cricket batsman & captain.

29th Apr– Daniel Day-Lewis, English actor.

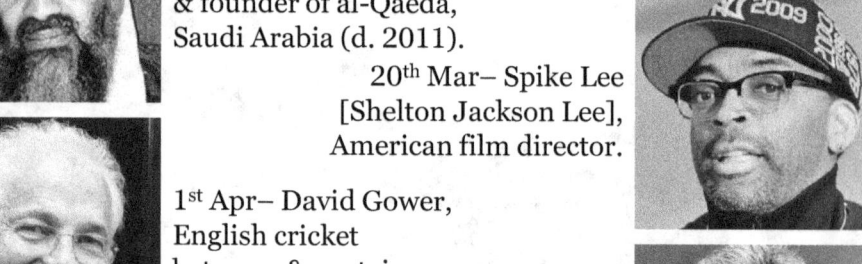

10th May– Sid Vicious [John Simon Ritchie], English musician (Sex Pistols) (d.1979).

13th May– Carrie Lam, Chinese politician, Chief Executive of Hong Kong (2017-2022).

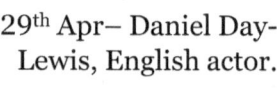

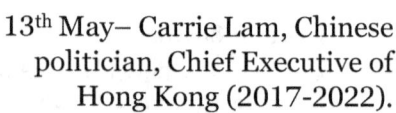

27th May– Siouxsie Sioux [Susan Ballion], British musician (Siouxsie & the Banshees).

12th Jun– Javed Miandad, Pakistani cricket captain.

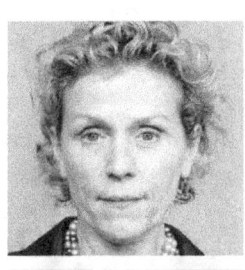

23rd Jun– Frances McDormand, American actress.

13th Jul– Cameron Crowe, American director, screenwriter, journalist, author & actor.

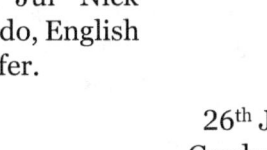

18th Jul– Nick Faldo, English golfer.

26th Jul– Wayne Grady, Australian golfer.

9th Aug– Melanie Griffith, American actress.

11th Aug– Masayoshi Son, Korean-Japanese (CEO SoftBank Mobile).

16th Aug– Tim Farriss, Australian musician (INXS).

24th Aug– Stephen Fry, English comedian, writer & actor.

27th Aug– Bernhard Langer, German golfer.

1st Sep– Gloria Estefan [Fajardo], Cuban-American singer.

28th Aug– Ai Weiwei, Chinese artist & activist.

14th Sep– Kepler Wessels, South African cricketer.

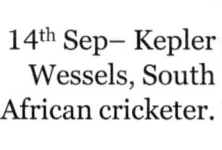

12th Sep– Rachel Ward, English-Australian actress.

30th Sep– Fran Drescher, American actress, author, activist, President SAG-AFTRA (2021-).

22nd Sep– Nick Cave, Australian singer-songwriter & author.

11th Oct– Dawn French, Welsh TV actress & comedian.

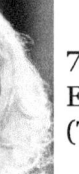

7th Oct– Jayne Torvill, English ice skater (Torvill & Dean).

4th Dec– Lee Smith, American Baseball Hall of Fame pitcher (7× MLB All-Star).

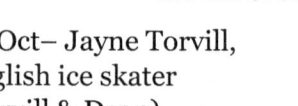

3rd Nov– Dolph Lundgren, Swedish actor, filmmaker, & martial artist.

9th Dec– Donny Osmond, American singer.

6th Dec– Andrew Cuomo, American politician & Governor of New York (2011-2021).

Schlitznic in the park
or a Schlitztogether in the open

Take your friends. Your picnic basket. Schlitz. Mix 'em all together–and you have a Schlitznic! On a nice, Schlitzsunny day there's nothing like it.

Today's Schlitz is adult refreshment. Paced to modern leisure. Sits light because it's Schlitzlight. You drink more of it without feeling full.

Now–have your Schlitnic with friends, Schlitzsnacks and Schlitz!

Schlitlight... kiss of hope   Schlitzkept... air-free   Schlitzness...continuous quality

Be a Schlitzer   Be refreshed

1957 in Numbers

Census Statistics [1]:

- Population of the world   2.87 billion
- Population in the United States   177.75 million
- Population in the United Kingdom   51.49 million
- Population in Canada   16.56 million
- Population in Australia   9.59 million
- Average age for marriage of women   20.3 years old
- Average age for marriage of men   22.6 years old
- Average family income USA $5,000 per year
- Minimum wage USA $1.00 per hour

Costs of Goods [2]:

- Average new house — $18,904
- Average new car — $2,100
- New Oldsmobile 88 Fiesta — $3,541
- A gallon of gasoline — $0.30
- A loaf of bread — $0.19
- A gallon of milk — $1.00
- Bacon — $0.49 per pound
- Potatoes, Maine Russet — $0.25 per 5 pounds
- Lamb, shoulder — $0.29 per pound
- Sliced Bacon — $0.49 per pound
- Soup, Campbells tomato can — $0.10
- Eggs — $0.55 per dozen
- Magazine, Woman's Day — $0.07
- Chewing gum — $0.19 per 6 packs

1 Figures taken from worldometers.info/world-population, US National Center for Health Statistics, Divorce and Divorce Rates US (cdc.gov/nchs/data/series/sr_21/sr21_029.pdf) and United States Census Bureau, Historical Marital Status Tables (census.gov/data/tables/time-series/demo/families/marital.html).
2 Figures from thepeoplehistory.com, mclib.info/reference/local-history & dqydj.com/historical-home-prices/.

Advertisement

You've got to hear it to believe it!
New General Electric Radio with Dual Speaker Musaphonic Sound - $39.95

Trouble with most *small* radios is they *sound* small. But here's a radio with a voice so true, so full, so rich—you've got to hear it to believe it! It's the all-new General Electric Radio that brings you Musaphonic Sound through Dual Speakers—a quality sound system never before available in a table radio. This multiple speaker principle is used in the costliest instruments you can buy. Sounds expensive. Looks expensive. Exclusively yours for $39.95 from General Electric—in choice of colors. Hear it this week!

Progress Is Our Most Important Product   General Electric

Advertisement

HAVE FUN ALL THE WAY

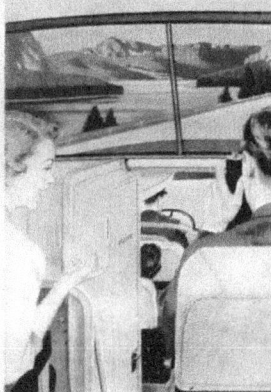

ENJOY AIR-CONDITIONED LUXURY! Off you go, free of your car, free of worry. Greyhound plans everything. Relax in easy-chair comfort...chat, read or take a nap.

STAY AT AMERICA'S TOP HOTELS. Greyhound experts do your planning, make reservations, arrange sight seeing side trips. Nothing for you to do but enjoy yourself!

SIGHT-SEE through sweeping, panoramic windows as Greyhound takes you along America's most scenic routes. Many Greyhounds have fully-equipped washrooms too!

For as low as $8 per day... leaving from any place ...Greyhound plans your complete trip, including transportation, hotel reservations, sight-seeing.

New! "Charge-A-Tour" plan! Travel now—pay later! Inquire today!

Imagine—a motoring vacation that begins the moment you're on the highway...that frees you from the work of driving, the problem of parking, and all the worry about what to see and where to stay. Sit back in a luxurious Greyhound and see America as it should be seen ...*close-up.* You choose the trip—Greyhound does the rest. Choose from hundreds of tours to the most exciting places in America. See Greyhound now or call your independent travel agent.

WATCH GREYHOUND'S STEVE ALLEN SHOW ON NBC-TV, SUNDAY NIGHTS

 *It's such a comfort to take the bus.*

Driving is no vacation!   Have fun all the way

Enjoy air-conditioned luxury! Off you go, free of your car, free of worry. Greyhound plans everything. Relax in easy-chair comfort...chat, read or take a nap.

Stay at America's top hotels. Greyhound experts do your planning, make reservations, arrange sight seeing side trips. Nothing for you to do but enjoy yourself!

Sight-see through sweeping, panoramic windows as Greyhound takes you along America's most scenic routes. Many Greyhounds have fully-equipped washrooms too!

For as low as $8 per day...leaving from any place...Greyhound plans your complete trip, including transportation, hotel reservations, sight-seeing.

New! "Charge-A-Tour" plan! Travel now–pay later! Inquire today!

Imagine—a motoring vacation that begins the moment you're on the highway...that frees you from the work of driving, the problem of parking, and all the worry about what to see and where to stay. Sit back in luxurious Greyhound and see America as it should be seen...*close-up.* You choose the trip–Greyhound does the rest. Choose from hundreds of tours to the most exciting places in America. See Greyhound now or call your independent travel agent.

Watch Greyhound's Steve Allen Show on NBC-TV, Sunday nights.

It's such a comfort to take the bus.

These words first appeared in print in the year 1957.

- OVERKILL
- Sputnik
- magic mushroom
- happy camper
- MULTICULTURALISM
- warts-and-all
- computerize
- Antiballistic missile
- scumbag
- paracetamol
- brain hormone
- TRANSSEXUAL
- moisturizer
- clip art
- one-hit wonder
- SMILEY FACE
- Leaf blower

*From merriam-webster.com/time-traveler/1957.

A heartfelt plea from the author:

I sincerely hope you enjoyed reading this book and that it brought back many fond memories from the past.

Success as an author has become increasingly difficult with the proliferation of **AI generated** copycat books by unscrupulous sellers. They are clever enough to escape copyright action and use dark web tactics to secure paid-for **fake reviews**, something I would never do.

Hence I would like to ask you — I plead with you — the reader, to leave a star rating or review on Amazon. This helps make my book discoverable for new readers, and helps me to compete fairly against the devious copycats.

If this book was a gift to you, you can leave stars or a review on your own Amazon account, or you can ask the gift-giver or a family member to do this on your behalf.

I have enjoyed researching and writing this book for you and would greatly appreciate your feedback.

Best regards,
Bernard Bradforsand-Tyler.

Please leave a
book review/rating at:

https://bit.ly/1957-reviews

Or scan the QR code:

Flashback books make the perfect gift-

https://bit.ly/FlashbackSeries

Image Attributions

Photographs and images used in this book are reproduced courtesy of the following:

Page 6 – California Zephyr 1957 print magazine advertisement, source: eBay (PD image).*
Page 8 – From *Life* magazine, 4th Mar 1957.
Source: books.google.com/books?id=rUEEAAAAMBAJ&printsec (PD image).*
Page 9 – Image cropped from the Gleem toothpaste advertisement in *Life* magazine 1st July 1957.
Source: books.google.com/books?id=ID8EAAAAMBAJ&printsec (PD image).*
Page 10 – Source: ushistoryscene.com/article/levittown/. Pre 1978, no copyright mark (PD image).
Page 11 – Images cropped from Gas Company and Gas Industry advert in *Life* magazine, 7th Oct 1957 and Westinghouse advert in *Life* magazine, 11th Mar 1957. Sources: books.google.com.sg/books?id=ZFYEAAAAMBAJ&printsec and books.google.com.sg/books?id=IEIEAAAAMBAJ&printsec (PD images).*
Page 12 – From *Life* magazine, 4th Mar 1957.
Source: books.google.com/books?id=rUEEAAAAMBAJ&printsec (PD image).*
Page 13 – TWA Jetstream 1957 print magazine advertisement, source: eBay (PD image).*
Page 14 – Trafalgar Square, July 1957, by Alfred Teske nach Foto von Karl Teske.
Source: commons.wikimedia.org/wiki/File:Trafalgar_Square_London_England_July_1957.jpg. Permission: GNU Free Documentation License.
Page 15 – Teenagers at a party, mid-'50s, private image, unknown creator. Pre 1978, no copyright mark (PD image). – Protestant graffiti in Belfast, Northern Ireland, Photo by George Garrigues / GeorgeLouis, Sept 1974. Source: commons.wikimedia.org/wiki/Category:Murals_in_Northern_Ireland. GNU Free Documentation License (PD image).
Page 16 – Cadillac ad from classiccarstodayonline.com/classic-car-print-advertisements/ (PD image).*
Page 17 – Image cropped from Champion Spark Plug ad printed in *Readers Digest* March 1956, source: flickr.com/photos/91591049@N00/12305118044/ by SenseiAlan. Attribution 4.0 Int (CC BY 4.0).
Page 18 – Big-Thrills Buick cropped ad from *Life* magazine, 17th June 1957. Source: books.google.com/books?id=Hj8EAAAAMBAJ&printsec. – Thrill-Power Plymouth '57 print advert. Source unknown. – '57 Chevrolet cropped advertissement. Source: abandonedcarsandtrucks.com (PD images).*
Page 19 – From *Life* magazine, 4th Mar 1957.
Source: books.google.com/books?id=rUEEAAAAMBAJ&printsec (PD image).*
Page 20 – From *Life* magazine, 14th Jan 1957.
Source: books.google.com/books?id=P1QEAAAAMBAJ&printsec (PD image).*
Page 21 – flickr.com/photos/tom-margie/1415312147/ Attribution-ShareAlike 4.0 International.
– MG Coupe print ad from 1957, source unknown. – Citroen ID19 print ad from 1957, source unknown.
– Chevrolet Assembly line, circa 1955. This image is the property of General Motors, printed here under fair use terms for information only, as it is significant to the article created. It is rendered in low resolution to avoid piracy. It is believed that this will not in any way limit the ability of the copyright owners to market or sell the product.
Page 22 – From *Life* magazine, 14th Oct 1957.
Source: books.google.com/books?id=m1YEAAAAMBAJ&printsec (PD image).*
Page 23 – '50s family, source: flickr.com/photos/95752929@N08/9018394774/. Attribution 4.0 (Creative Commons (CC) by 4.0).
– *The Danny Thomas Show*, source: en.wikipedia.org/wiki/The_Danny_Thomas_Show. (PD image).**
Page 24 – *Gunsmoke*, 1958 promotion photo by CBS.**
Source: en.wikipedia.org/wiki/Gunsmoke#Television_series_ (1955–1975). – *General Electric Theatre*, 1955 by CBS.** Source: en.wikipedia.org/wiki/General_Electric_Theater.
Page 25 – *Have Gun will Travel* screen still by CBS 24th Jun 1960.** Source: commons.wikimedia.org/wiki/Category:Have_Gun_–_Will_Travel. – *Wagon Train* publicity image by NBC. 30th Mar 1958. Source: commons.wikimedia.org/wiki/Category:Wagon_Train. – *Perry Mason* screen still from 21st Sep 1957 premier episode.** Source: en.wikipedia.org/wiki/Perry_Mason_(1957_TV_series). – *The Lucy-Desi Comedy Hour* screen still from 6th Nov 1957 premier episode.**
Source: commons.wikimedia.org/wiki/Category:The_Lucy–Desi_Comedy_Hour.
Page 26 – From *Life* magazine, 16th Dec 1957.
Source: books.google.com/books?id=1FUEAAAAMBAJ&printsec (PD image).*
Page 27 – Images of *Operation Plumbbob* in the Nevada Deseret, 1957. All images property of National Nuclear Security Administration. Nevada Site Office Photo Library under numbers PLU-57-100, PLU-57-031 and PLU-57-037 (PD images).
Page 28 – From *Life* magazine, 1st Apr 1957.
Source: books.google.com/books?id=7kwEAAAAMBAJ&printsec (PD image).*
Page 29 – Romanian stamp, 1957. Source: commons.wikimedia.org/wiki/Category:Laika. (PD image).
Page 30 – Crowd at the Lincoln Memorial 17th May 1957. Photographer unknown. Courtesy of the US Library of Congress, Reproduction Number: LC-USZ62-126522. – Martin Luther King Jnr, by Warren K. Leffler, Courtesy of the US Library of Congress, digital ID loc.gov/pictures/resource/ppmsca.49864/. Pre 1978, no mark (PD image).
Page 31 – NY City Mayor greeting Little Rock 9, by Walter Albertin. Courtesy of the US Library of Congress, Reproduction Number: LC-USZ62-125125. – 101st Airborne Division escort African American Students, 25th Sept 1957. Still image taken from Operation Arkansas, Little Rock, Arkansas news footage

by the US Department of Defense, courtesy of National Archives at College Park - Motion Pictures (RDSM), National Archives Identifier: 27642, Local Identifier:111-LC-41036.
– Rally at State Capitol, 20th Aug 1959. Courtesy of the US Library of Congress, Reproduction Number: LC-DIG-ppmsca-03120. All images pre 1978 (PD images).
Page 32 – Airline posters from 1957. Copyright is most likely owned by either the publisher or the creator of the work. These posters are reproduced for information only under fair use terms. The images are rendered in low resolution to avoid piracy. It is believed these images will not in any way limit the ability of the copyright owner to sell their product. Pre 1978, no copyright mark (PD image).*
Page 33 – From *Life* magazine, 11th Nov 1957.
Source: books.google.com/books?id=tVYEAAAAMBAJ&printsec (PD image).*
Page 34 – Photo and poster from the Irish Republican & Marxist History Project. Pre 1978, no copyright mark (PD image).
Page 35 – From *Life* magazine, 2nd Dec 1957.
Source: books.google.com/books?id=j1YEAAAAMBAJ&printsec (PD image).*
Page 36 & 37 – Propaganda posters for the Hundred Flowers movement, by the Chinese Communist Party (PD image).** – Mao on an airplane in 1957. Source: commons.wikimedia.org/wiki/Category:Mao_Zedong_in_1957 (PD image). – Arrest of a Rightist, creator unknown.
Source: alphahistory.com/chineserevolution/hundred-flowers-campaign/.
Page 38 – From *Life* magazine, 1st Apr 1957.
Source: books.google.com/books?id=7kwEAAAAMBAJ&printsec (PD image).*
Page 39 – From *Life* magazine, 11th Feb 1957.
Source: books.google.com/books?id=BVQEAAAAMBAJ&printsec (PD image).*
Page 40 – Hudson, August 1954 by Universal. Source: commons.wikimedia.org/wiki/Category:Rock_Hudson. – Wayne, publicity photo, 1952. Source: commons.wikimedia.org/wiki/Category:John_Wayne_in_1952. – Novak for *New York Sunday News* in 1957, source: commons.wikimedia.org/wiki/Category:Kim_Novak. – Deneuve 1969 from *The April Fools*. Source: commons.wikimedia.org/wiki/Category:Catherine_Deneuve. All images pre 1978, no copyright mark (PD image).
Page 41 – *Search for Paradise* movie poster, 1957, by Cinerama Releasing Corp.** Source: en.wikipedia.org/wiki/Search_for_Paradise. – *Sayonara* movie poster, 1957, by Warner Bros.** Source: en.wikipedia.org/wiki/Sayonara 6. – *Island in the Sun* movie poster, 1957, by 20th Century Fox.**
Page 42 – Screen still & movie poster from *The Bridge on the River Kwai*, 1957 by Columbia Pictures.**
Page 43 – Screen stills *A Farewell to Arms* (20th Century Fox,** and *Battle Hymn* (Universal Pictures).**
Page 44 – From *Life* Magazine, 21st Jan 1957.
Source: books.google.com/books?id=PFQEAAAAMBAJ&printsec (PD image).*
Page 45 – Seuss drawing the Grinch, by Al Ravenna, World Telegram staff photographer. From the US Library of Congress, digital ID: cph.3c24309. Pre-1978, no copyright mark (PD image). – Copyright for book cover art is most likely owned by either the publisher or the creator of the work. These covers are for information only and are reproduced under fair use terms. The images are rendered in low resolution to avoid piracy. It is believed these images will not in any way limit the ability of the copyright owner to sell their product.
Page 46 – From *Life* Magazine, 19th Aug 1957.
Source: books.google.com/books?id=Kj8EAAAAMBAJ&printsec (PD image).*
Page 47 – Photos from the original Broadway production of *West Side Story*, 1957.**
Source: commons.wikimedia.org/ wiki/Category:West_Side_Story.
Page 48 – From *Life* Magazine, 6th May 1957.
Source: books.google.com/books?id=KD8EAAAAMBAJ&printsec (PD image).*
Page 49 – Chuck Berry publicity photo by Universal Attractions, 1957. Source: commons.wikimedia.org/wiki/Category:Chuck_Berry. – Fats Domino in Amsterdam by Hugo van Gelderen / Anefo, 3rd Nov 1962. Copyright holder National Archives, CC0. Access number 2.24.01.05, Part number 914-4772. (CC0 PD image). – Lewis, source: en.wikipedia.org/wiki/Jerry_Lee_Lewis. – Sun Records, source: commons.wikimedia.org/wiki/File:Sun_Studio,_Memphis.jpg. All photos this page pre-1978, no mark (PD image).
Page 50 – Elvis Presley, date unknown. Source: commons.wikimedia.org/wiki/File:Elvispresleycolorful pic.jpg by Arbresha12. Attribution-Share Alike 4.0 International License. – Boone, circa 1960. Source: en.wikipedia.org/wiki/Pat_Boone. Pre 1978, no copyright mark (PD image). – Perry Como by NBC Television, 1956. Source: commons.wikimedia.org/wiki/File:Perry_Como_1956.JPG. PD-PRE1978 (PD image). – Debbie Reynolds publicity photo, circa 1964. Source: http://weheartvintage.co/2013/02/20/debbie-reynolds-in-a-red-fur-coat/t. Pre 1978, no copyright mark (PD image).
Page 51 – The Everly Brothers publicity photo by Cadence Records, 1958.
Source: commons.wikimedia.org/wiki/Category: The_Everly_Brothers. Pre 1978, no copyright (PD image). – Belafonte, from the Carl Van Vechten photograph collection (Library of Congress), 18th Feb 1954. Source: loc.gov/item/2004662591/.LOC control number 2004662591 (PD image).
Page 52 – Elvis Presley in St. Louis March 1957, with some local fans. April/May 1957.
Source: elvispresleymusic.com.au/ elvis-presley-1957.html. Pre 1978, no copyright mark (PD image).
Page 53 – Graceland by Abbie Myers, 2nd Nov 2006. Source: commons.wikimedia.org/wiki/Category: Graceland_Mansion. Attribution CC BY-SA 4.0. – Elvis at Radio Recorders, Hollywood, CA. April/May 1957. Source: elvispresleymusic.com.au/elvis-presley-1957.html. Pre 1978, no mark (PD image).
Page 54 – From *Life* magazine, 4th Mar 1957.
Source: books.google.com/books?id=KFQEAAAAMBAJ&printsec (PD image).*

Page 55 – Dresses from the *Sears Roebuck Home Order Catalog,* Summer 1957. (PD image).*
Page 56 – Images from myvintagevogue.com. Pre 1978, no copyright mark (PD image).
Page 57 – Dior's New Look, sketches by author. – Models wear Christian Dior, 1955. Creators unknown. Pre 1978, no copyright mark (PD image).
Page 58 – Bullet Bra From *Life* Magazine, 4th June 1956. Source: books.google.com.sg/books?id=oEgEAAAAMBAJ&printsec. (PD image).* – Advertisement for Toni Todd dresses, source: *Charm Magazine*, January 1955. (PD image).*
Page 59 – From *Life* Magazine, 8th Apr 1957. Source: books.google.com/books?id=8EwEAAAAMBAJ&printsec (PD image).*
Page 60 – Dresses from the Sears and Roebucks Spring Catalog, 1957. (PD image).*
Page 61 – From *Life* magazine, 4th Mar 1957. Source: books.google.com/books?id=rUEEAAAAMBAJ&printsec (PD image).*
Page 62 – From *Life* Magazine, 28th Mar 1955. Source: books.google.com/books?id=FlQEAAAAMBAJ&printsec. – Dress patterns, source: sovintagepatterns.com/VINTAGE-PATTERNS-1950s_c_13-6-4.html. – Monroe, publicity photo from *The Prince and the Showgirl* by Milton H. Greene/Warner Bros, source: commons.wikimedia.org/wiki/Category:Marilyn_Monroe_in_1957. All images pre-1978 (PD image).
Page 63 – Sinatra, source: morrisonhotelgallery.com/collections/wtvp8g/The-Sinatra-Experience-. – Brando, source: dailybreak.co/wp-content/uploads/2019/06/Marlon-Brando-Ford-Thunderbird-1955-Est.-2444.jpg. – Presley, source: commons.wikimedia.org/wiki/Category:Elvis_Presley_in_1958. All images this page pre-1978, no mark (PD image).
Page 64 – From *Life* Magazine, 10th Jun 1957. Source: books.google.com/books?id=Nz8EAAAAMBAJ&printsec (PD image).*
Page 65 – Darlene Hard and Althea Gibson, 6th Jul 1957, creator unknown. Source: commons.wikimedia.org/wiki/Category: 1957_Wimbledon_Championships. – Suggs, circa 1958. Creator unknown. Source: commons.wikimedia.org/wiki/Category:Louise_Suggs. – Fangio, Grand Prix win at Netherlands, by Harry Anefo 19th Jun 1955 . From the National Archives of Netherlands. Number access: 2.24.01.04. Item number: 907-1901. All images this page pre-1978, no mark (PD image).
Page 66 – From *Life* Magazine, 10th Jun 1957. Source: books.google.com/books?id=Nz8EAAAAMBAJ&printsec (PD image).*
Page 67 – Shippingport Atomic Power Station courtesy of Pittsburgh Post-Gazette Interactive – Professor Donald, creator unknown. Source: ob-ultrasound.net/iandonaldbio.html. All images this page pre-1978, no mark (PD image).
Page 68 – Macmillan by Cecil W. Stoughton. Source: commons.wikimedia.org/wiki/Category:Harold_Macmillan. – Morrison with Pluto Platter, from Connecticut State Library, creator unknown. Source: commons.wikimedia.org/wiki/File:Walter_Frederick_Morrison.jpg. – Onassis by Pieter Jongerhuis from the National Archives of Netherlands ID: 920-8103. All images this page pre-1978, no mark (PD image).
Page 69 – Loren and Ponti in Copenhagen, 21st Jan 1958, creator unknown. Source: commons.wikimedia.org/wiki/Category:Sophia_Loren_in_1958. – Eisenhower portrait 1959, creator unknown. Source: commons.wikimedia.org/wiki/Dwight_D._Eisenhower. – Duvalier 1957, creator unknown. Source: commons.wikimedia.org/wiki/Category:François_Duvalier. – Lewisham crash, creator unkown. All images this page pre-1978, no mark (PD image).
Page 70 – From *Life* magazine, 5th Aug 1957. Source: books.google.com/books?id=Lj8EAAAAMBAJ&printsec (PD image).*
Page 71 – From *Life* magazine, 14th Oct 1957. Source: books.google.com/books?id=m1YEAAAAMBAJ&printsec (PD image).*
Page 72-74 – All photos are, where possible, CC BY 2.0 or PD images made available by the creator for free use including commercial use. Where commercial use photos are unavailable, photos are included here for information only under U.S. fair use laws due to: 1- images are low resolution copies; 2- images do not devalue the ability of the copyright holders to profit from the original works in any way; 3- Images are too small to be used to make illegal copies for use in another book; 4- The images are relevant to the article created.
Page 75 – From *Life* magazine, 3rd Jun 1957. Source: books.google.com/books?id=Nj8EAAAAMBAJ&printsec. (PD image).*
Page 78 – General Electric Musaphonic 1957 print magazine advertisement, source: eBay (PD image).*
Page 79 – Greyhound bus 1957 print magazine advertisement, source: eBay (PD image).*
*Advertisement (or image from an advertisement) is in the public domain because it was published in a collective work (such as a periodical issue) in the US between 1925 and 1977 and without a copyright notice specific to the advertisement.
**Posters for movies or events are either in the public domain (published in the US between 1925 and 1977 and without a copyright notice specific to the artwork) or owned by the production company, creator, or distributor of the movie or event. Posters, where not in the public domain, and screen stills from movies or TV shows, are reproduced here under USA Fair Use laws due to: 1- images are low resolution copies; 2- images do not devalue the ability of the copyright holders to profit from the original works in any way; 3- Images are too small to be used to make illegal copies for use in another book; 4- The images are relevant to the article created.

This book was written by Bernard Bradforsand-Tyler as part of *A Time Traveler's Guide* series of books.

All rights reserved. The author exerts the moral right to be identified as the author of the work.

No parts of this book may be reproduced, stored in any retrieval system, or transmitted in any form or by any means, without prior written permission from the author.

This is a work of nonfiction. No names have been changed, no events have been fabricated. The content of this book is provided as a source of information for the reader, however it is not meant as a substitute for direct expert opinion. Although the author has made every effort to ensure that the information in this book is correct at time of printing, and while this publication is designed to provide accurate information in regard to the subject matters covered, the author assumes no responsibility for errors, inaccuracies, omissions, or any other inconsistencies herein and hereby disclaims any liability to any party for any loss, damage, or disruption caused by errors or omissions.

All images contained herein are reproduced with the following permissions:
- Images included in the public domain.
- Images obtained under creative commons license.
- Images included under fair use terms.
- Images reproduced with owner's permission.

All image attributions and source credits are provided at the back of the book. All images are the property of their respective owners and are protected under international copyright laws.

First printed in 2022 in the USA (ISBN 978-1-922676-05-4) and 2024 (ISBN 978-1-922676-14-6).
Revised in 2024, 2nd Edition (ISBN 978-1-922676-16-0).
Self-published by B. Bradforsand-Tyler.

www.ingramcontent.com/pod-product-compliance
Lightning Source LLC
Chambersburg PA
CBHW072104110526
44590CB00018B/3311